Concert and Contest COLLECTION

Compiled and Edited
by **H. VOXMAN**

for

Solo Baritone (Bass Clef)

B♭ Cornet, Trumpet or Baritone with Piano Accompaniment

CONTENTS

RUBANK

HAL•LEONARD CORPORATION
7777 W. BLUEMOUND RD. P.O. BOX 13819 MILWAUKEE, WI 53213

Sarabanda and Gavotta

Baritone 𝄢

A. CORELLI
Edited by H. Voxman

© Copyright MCMLXII by Rubank, Inc., Chicago, Ill.
International Copyright Secured

Dedication
(Zueignung)

Baritone 𝄢

RICHARD STRAUSS, Op. 10, No. 1
Transcribed by H. Voxman

© Copyright MCMLXII by Rubank, Inc., Chicago, Ill.
International Copyright Secured

Premier Solo de Concours

Baritone ♯

RENÉ MANIET
Edited by H. Voxman

© Copyright MCMLXII by Rubank, Inc., Chicago, Ill.
International Copyright Secured

Calm As the Night

Baritone 𝄢

CARL BÖHM
Edited by H. Voxman

© Copyright MCMLXII by Rubank, Inc., Chicago, Ill.
International Copyright Secured

Andante and Allegro

Baritone 𝄢

ROBERT CLÉRISSE
Edited by H. Voxman

© Copyright MCMLXII by Rubank, Inc., Chicago, Ill.
International Copyright Secured

Romance in Eb

Baritone 𝄢

LEROY OSTRANSKY

© Copyright MCMLXII by Rubank, Inc., Chicago, Ill.
International Copyright Secured

Air Gai

Baritone 𝄢

G. P. BERLIOZ
Edited by H. Voxman

© Copyright MCMLXII by Rubank, Inc., Chicago, Ill.
International Copyright Secured

Baritone 𝄢

Orientale

Baritone 𝄢

J. Ed. BARAT
Edited by H. Voxman

© Copyright MCMLXII by Rubank, Inc., Chicago, Ill.
International Copyright Secured

Élégie

Baritone ℈

ALEXANDRE J. DUQUESNE
Edited by H. Voxman

triple tongue [ad lib.]

© Copyright MCMLXII by Rubank, Inc., Chicago, Ill.
International Copyright Secured

Serenade

Baritone

OSKAR BÖHME, Op. 22, No. 1
Edited by H. Voxman

© Copyright MCMLXII by Rubank, Inc., Chicago, Ill.
International Copyright Secured

My Regards

Baritone 𝄢

EDWARD LLEWELLYN
Edited by H. Voxman

© Copyright MCMLXII by Rubank, Inc., Chicago, Ill.
International Copyright Secured

L'Allegro
(The Merry Man)

Baritone 𝄢

PAUL KOEPKE

© Copyright MCMLXII by Rubank, Inc., Chicago, Ill.
International Copyright Secured

Petite Pièce Concertante

Baritone 𝄢

GUILLAUME BALAY
Edited by H. Voxman

© Copyright MCMLXII by Rubank, Inc., Chicago, Ill.
International Copyright Secured

Morceau de Concours

Baritone

G. ALARY, Op. 57
Edited by H. Voxman

© Copyright MCMLXII by Rubank, Inc., Chicago, Ill.
International Copyright Secured

Concertino

Baritone 𝄢

LEROY OSTRANSKY

© Copyright MCMLXII by Rubank, Inc., Chicago, Ill.
International Copyright Secured

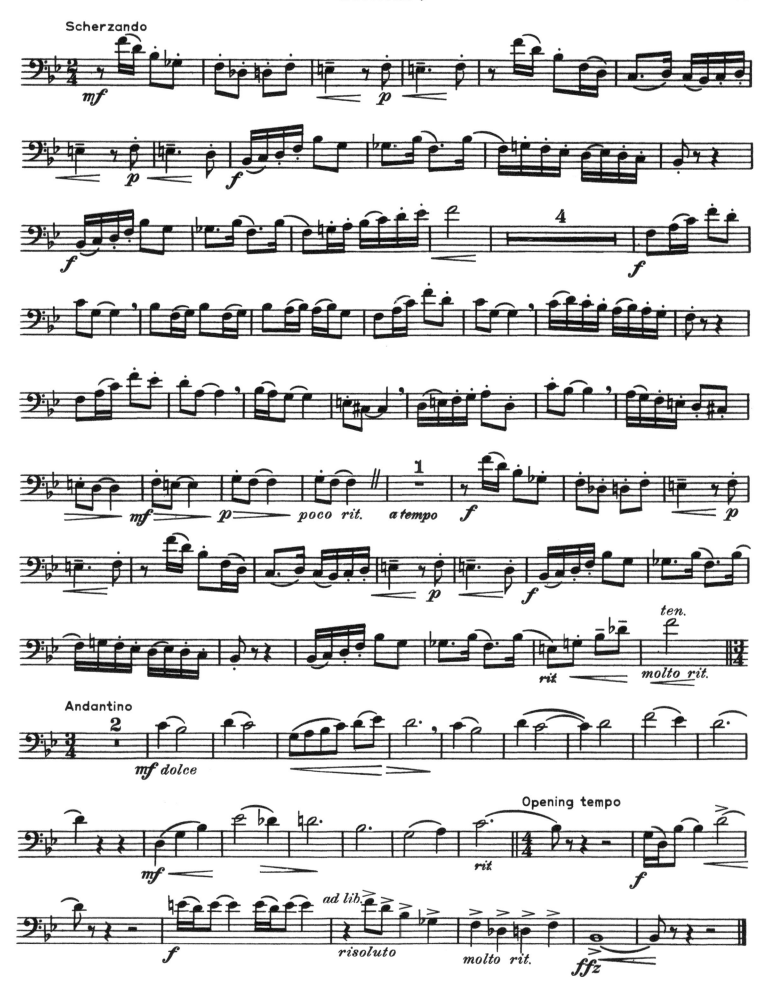

Andante
from Concerto in Eb

Baritone 𝄢

F. J. HAYDN
Edited by H. Voxman

© Copyright MCMLXII by Rubank, Inc., Chicago, Ill.
International Copyright Secured